Devon Missed the Joke

Written By
Jo Oliver-Yeager, MS

Other Books By Jo Oliver-Yeager

Sophie Counts Her Steps
Adam (Sometimes) Can't Sit Still

Copyright © 2021 Kind Words Publishing
ISBN 978-1-7358815-4-6

All rights reserved. This book may not be reproduced in whole or in part in any form, or by any means, without express written permission from the publisher.

Published by:

Kind Words Publishing
kindwordspublishing@gmail.com

This is dedicated to all the wonderful people with Autism.

This book is one in a series intended to educate people about acceptance and understanding as well as giving a voice to anyone who may not fit into that "neat little box."

For my wonderful Tony and the inspiration of my three babies who hold my heart- Nyan, Tessa, & Auden for always supporting my love of writing.

Devon enjoys building with LEGO bricks.

He REALLY enjoys building with LEGO bricks.

He rarely looks at the directions to construct elaborate creations. Sometimes, he can spend all day building a spaceship or submarine.

Sometimes, he struggles until his creations are exactly up to his standard.

When his parents call him down for dinner there can be struggles. He has a hard time stopping in the middle of his process.

In fact, if dad comes up a minute or two before dinner time, it may cause Devon to feel frustrated which could end in tears.

Devon's best friend, Riley, has been friends with Devon since they were both in preschool.

Building friendships wasn't always easy for Devon. Sometimes the kids at school were not as understanding.

Devon has Autism.

He can sometimes miss the subtle conversations. He could also get overwhelmed and have to leave the classroom.

Another thing that stood out for Devon was that he had a teacher's aide in class. Margaret had been Devon's aide since kindergarten.

Now in 3rd grade, he needed Margaret, but he was also managing better on his own.

Many of his classmates supported Devon if he struggled during class or recess. But one day a new student started in the 3rd grade.

Thomas had transferred to Devon's school. Thomas was a funny kid. He liked to pull jokes on his classmates. Devon didn't understand Thomas.

He asked his mom why Thomas needed to be goofy in class. Devon's mom explained it could be because Thomas is new and wants to be liked.

One day, Thomas joked with Devon and expected him to laugh. "What happened to the two birds who fell from their nest?" asked Thomas.

Devon looked at him and responded in a logical manner and repeated the question with a question.

"What would two birds do if they fell from the nest? Wouldn't they die?" Devon wanted to know. Thomas looked at Devon and seemed confused.

Margaret sat back and watched, ready to help.

Devon looked at Thomas and said, "Oh, this was a joke? I am not always good at picking up on jokes. I have Autism." Thomas didn't know what Autism was so he asked Devon to explain.

Devon explained that having Autism, for him, means he can miss things sometimes. He can get overwhelmed and could scream in class if he is upset.

He also pointed to Margaret so that Thomas knew who she was and why she was there.

That day in math, the nurse came into the classroom to get a student who was leaving early for an appointment. The door opened and interrupted the lesson.

Devon started yelling and covering his ears. He was very stressed because he had not expected the interruption.

Thomas looked around to see how the other kids were responding. When he saw that no one was concerned, he went back to his workbook.

Margaret got up from her spot in the back of the class and encouraged Devon to stay calm or he could go for a walk if he needed.

The more Thomas learned about Devon, the more understanding he became. He also found that he liked playing with Devon.

Thomas liked how fast Devon could finish a puzzle and create things in art class. Thomas wasn't good at art. He wanted to sit near Devon because he hoped he could help him with his project.

Devon, though, wasn't comfortable having people sit too close to him and had to ask Thomas to move over a bit.

The next day, the class went on a field trip to the museum.

The students were put into groups of four. Devon's group consisted of Riley, Jasmine, and Thomas. Thomas was fitting into class well.

As they walked through the museum, Devon pointed out all the paintings that were by Van Gogh. He had memorized each one from an art book he owned.

Thomas shouted out, "but where did the 'Van Go'?" Riley and Jasmine laughed.

Devon looked at Thomas and said 'That was a joke, right?"

Thomas laughed, "Yes Devon, that was a joke." Devon smiled.

He didn't miss the joke that time.

Devon was getting better at picking up on Thomas' joking and liked having another good friend.

Learning about a person's differences can help you to see what you have in common.

Resources

- Autism Speaks
  https://www.autismspeaks.org/

- Autism Society of America
  http://www.autism-society.org/

- American Autism Association
  https://www.myautism.org/

- The Autism Research Institute
  https://www.autism.org/

- Association for Science in Autism Treatment
  https://asatonline.org/

- The Arc: Autism Now
  https://autismnow.org/

www.ingramcontent.com/pod-product-compliance
Lightning Source LLC
Chambersburg PA
CBHW051304110526
44589CB00025B/2937